Grammar Jingles™
Primary

Harcourt

Orlando   Boston   Dallas   Chicago   San Diego

Visit *The Learning Site!*
www.harcourtschool.com

Table of Contents

Grammar Jingles™ Chart

Grade 1

Chapter 1	**Track 1:** Good Sense! (sentences)
Chapter 2	**Track 2:** Who Did What? (parts of a sentence)
Chapter 3	**Track 3:** You Ask, I'll Tell (statements and questions)
Chapter 4	**Track 3:** You Ask, I'll Tell (statements and questions)
Chapter 6	**Track 4:** Name It! (nouns and possessives)
Chapter 7	**Track 4:** Name It! (nouns and possessives)
Chapter 8	**Track 4:** Name It! (nouns and possessives)
Chapter 9	**Track 5:** And *S* Makes More (plurals)
Chapter 11	**Track 8:** Likes and Wishes (verb endings)
Chapter 12	**Track 8:** Likes and Wishes (verb endings)
Chapter 13	**Track 9:** What Happened? (past tense)
Chapter 14	**Track 10:** All About Being (the verb be)
Chapter 16	**Track 12:** Tell Me More (describing words)
Chapter 17	**Track 12:** Tell Me More (describing words)
Chapter 18	**Track 12:** Tell Me More (describing words)
Chapter 19	**Track 15:** Big and Small (comparing)
Chapter 21	**Track 6:** Properly Named (proper nouns)
Chapter 22	**Track 6:** Properly Named (proper nouns)
Chapter 23	**Track 7:** He Is He, I Am Me (pronouns)
Chapter 24	**Track 7:** He Is He, I Am Me (pronouns)
Chapter 26	**Track 1:** Good Sense! (sentences)
Chapter 27	**Track 1:** Good Sense! (sentences)
Chapter 28	**Track 24:** Two, Too, To (easily confused words)
Chapter 29	**Track 24:** Two, Too, To (easily confused words)

Grammar Jingles™ Chart

Grade 2

Chapter 1	**Track 1:** Good Sense! (sentences)
Chapter 2	**Track 2:** Who Did What? (parts of a sentence)
Chapter 4	**Track 3:** You Ask, I'll Tell (statements and questions)
Chapter 5	**Track 3:** You Ask, I'll Tell (statements and questions)
Chapter 7	**Track 4:** Name It! (nouns and possessives)
Chapter 8	**Track 5:** And *S* Makes More (plurals)
Chapter 10	**Track 6:** Properly Named (proper nouns)
Chapter 11	**Track 7:** He Is He, I Am Me (pronouns)
Chapter 13	**Track 8:** Likes and Wishes (verb endings)
Chapter 14	**Track 9:** What Happened? (past tense)
Chapter 16	**Track 10:** All About Being (the verb *be*)
Chapter 17	**Track 11:** Have, Has, Had (agreement with *have, has, had*)
Chapter 19	**Track 12:** Tell Me More (describing words)
Chapter 20	**Track 12:** Tell Me More (describing words) **Track 13:** Pick and Choose (synonyms)
Chapter 22	**Track 12:** Tell Me More (describing words) **Track 14:** An Apple or a Peach? (*a* and *an*)
Chapter 23	**Track 15:** Big and Small (comparing) **Track 10:** All About Being (the verb *be*)
Chapter 25	**Track 16:** Come Running (irregular verbs) **Track 17:** Join In! (comma with *and*)
Chapter 26	**Track 18:** See, Saw (using *go, do, see*)
Chapter 28	**Track 19:** Helpers (helping verbs)
Chapter 29	**Track 20:** How and Where (adverbs)
Chapter 31	**Track 7:** He Is He, I Am Me (pronouns)
Chapter 32	**Track 21:** Letters Out, Apostrophes In (contractions)
Chapter 34	**Track 22:** First, Next, Last (comma after introductory words) **Track 23:** Pause Here (commas)
Chapter 35	**Track 24:** Two, Too, To (easily confused words)

Good Sense!

(chorus)   When you put some words together
To tell a particular thought,
If the words make sense, it's a **sentence**.
If they don't make sense, it's not.

I caught a very big . . . .
Does not tell what I caught.
I caught a very big fish.
And that completes the thought.

(chorus)

I swim like pool at the to
Does not make sense to me.
I like to swim at the pool.
Is what it's supposed to be.

(chorus)

Who Did What?

(chorus)   Let's make sentences together.
I'll name the **what** or the **who**,
And the part that tells **what happens**
Will be the part for you.

A fox . . . was looking at some chickens.
The chickens . . . clucked, "No, no!"
The farmer . . . came out running.
The fox. . . was told to GO!

(chorus)

Some pigs . . . were building little houses.
One house . . . was made of sticks.
A wolf . . . blew it down in a minute.
That pig . . . now builds with bricks.

(chorus)

You Ask, I'll Tell

(chorus) Ask me a **question**.
What will I do?
I'll tell you the answer
In a **statement** or two.

What is your favorite color?
My favorite color is blue.
I also like green and purple and yellow
And red and orange, too.

(chorus)

What shall we play with at recess?
You take the softball and bat.
And I'll take a soccer ball, marbles,
and jump rope
To play with after that!

(chorus)

Name It!

Where am I going?
What will I see?
Nouns can name those things for me.
How can I show you whose it will be?
Add **s** after an **apostrophe**.

I'm going to the **market**
To buy some frozen **peas**,
Some **carrots** and **bananas**,
And my **sister's** favorite **cheese**.

(chorus)

I'm going to a **circus**
To see a funny **clown**,
And **elephants** and **tigers**
On my **cousin's** side of **town**.

(chorus)

And *S* Makes More

(chorus)

To make a noun plural
Add **es** or **s**.
That changes the meaning
To more and not less.

Just add **s** to apple,
And keep one for you.
Add **es** to sandwich.
You'll have lunch for two.

(chorus)

Just add **s** to candle
On top of your cake.
Add **es** for wishes
That you're going to make.

(chorus)

Properly Named

(chorus)
Names and months,
Streets and towns,
Have capital letters
To make **proper nouns**.

My mother's name is **Mari**.
My father's name is **Bill**.
I live on **Little River Road**
In the town of **Windy Hill**.

(chorus)

My sister's name is **Nina**.
Her birthday is today.
But mine is in another month.
I have to wait 'til **May**.

(chorus)

Grammar Jingles™ • Primary

He Is He, I Am Me

(chorus)

Instead of his name, say **he**.
Instead of her name, say **she**.
Use **it** to take the place of a thing.
For yourself, use **I** or **me**.

Carl is my cousin.
He lives far away.
He sent **me** a book.
I got **it** today.

(chorus)

I drew a picture
Of Jenny and Jed.
"**It** really looks
Like **us**," **they** said.

(chorus)

Likes and Wishes

(chorus)   A verb can tell what someone does,
But notice when you read,
Some verbs add **s** or **es**.
Some verbs have all they need.

I **like** to swing up high.
My father **pushes** me
'Til I **look** over the playground fence
To **see** what I can **see**.

(chorus)

I **wish** I had an airplane.
My sister **wants** a horse.
We can **choose** the ones we **want**
When we **grow** up, of course.

(chorus)

What Happened?

(chorus)
When you want to tell a story,
Your verbs will need **ed**
When you write what **happened**
Or when you talk to me.

A billy goat **walked** upon a bridge.
A troll said, "Go away!"
The goat just **wanted** grass to eat
And **trotted** on his way.

(chorus)

A mother bear **cooked** porridge.
The baby's was just right.
A girl **walked** in and ate it up
When they were out of sight.

(chorus)

All About Being

(chorus)
Am and **is** are verbs about being,
Were and **was** about been.
I make sure the verbs I'm using
Make sense in the sentence they're in.

I wouldn't say, "I **is** his cousin."
I would say, "I **am**."
I wouldn't say, "He **are** my brother."
He **is** my brother Sam.

(chorus)

I wouldn't say, "I **were** the pitcher."
"I **was** the pitcher," I'd say.
I wouldn't say, "We **was** the winners."
We **were** the winners today.

(chorus)

Have, Has, Had

(chorus) The words **have**, **has**, and **had**
Are verbs that must agree
With the naming part of the sentence,
Like **I** or **he** or **she**.

I **had** a little kitten.
Now I **have** a cat.
I **had** a pretty red balloon.
It broke, and that was that.

(chorus)

Lori **has** a pencil box.
I **have** pencils, too.
She **has** lots of pencils,
But I **have** only two!

(chorus)

Describing Words

(chorus)
To make my writing special
And enjoyable to read,
Describing words that tell a lot
Are surely what I need.

Is this flower just a flower?
No, it smells **sweet** and it's **pink**.
And the petals are as **smooth** and **soft**
As baby hands, I think.

(chorus)

Is an ocean just an ocean
Where you go to swim and play?
No, it's **blue** and **green** with **shiny**
    bubbles
Changing every day.

(chorus)

Pick and Choose

(chorus)

Describing words can be alike,
So I can pick and choose
From several close in meaning
And decide the one to use.

A baby bird is **small**.
Or is it **itty-bitty**?
A picture can be **beautiful**.
Or is it very **pretty**?

(chorus)

Carrot cake is **sugary**.
Or is it very **sweet**?
Bananas are **delicious**.
Or are they a **tasty** treat?

(chorus)

An Apple or a Peach?

(chorus)

Use **an** if the next word starts with **a**
Or **i** or **u** or **o** or **e**.
Use **a** if it's a consonant
Like **b** or **d** or **t**.

An apple is **a** special treat.
I like to hear it crunch.
An apple makes **a** nice dessert.
I'll take one with my lunch.

(chorus)

Or shall I take **a** peach today
So juicy and so sweet?
A peach or **an** apple would be good.
Which one shall I eat?

(chorus)

Grammar Jingles™ • Primary

Big and Small

(chorus)

How is this thing
Different from that?
Which is **bigger**,
A lion or cat?

A rabbit is small.
A mouse is **smaller**.
A camel is tall.
A giraffe is **taller**.

(chorus)

My mother is short.
My brother is tall.
My father is
The **tallest** of all.

(chorus)

Come Running

(chorus) To use the verbs **come**, **run**, and **give**,
Think, was it then or is it now?
How should I use **came**, **ran**,
  and **gave**?
Good sense will tell me how.

I **come** to school five days a week.
I **run** in relay races.
I **give** my friends birthday gifts.
To bring smiles to their faces.

(chorus)

I **came** to school last Friday
And **gave** my show-and-tell.
I **ran** out to the playground
When I heard the recess bell.

(chorus)

Join In!

(chorus)
To join two sentences together
When the second one tells more,
Put **and** between the sentences,
And use a comma before.

We went to a museum,
    and we sang songs on the bus.
A woman met us at the door,
    and she gave a talk for us.

(chorus)

We went into a gallery,
    and we saw a bowl of gold.
It came from ancient Egypt,
    and it was very old.

(chorus)

See, Saw

(chorus)   If I **go** and **do** and **see**,
When I get home I'll say
I **went** and **did** and **saw**
As I tell about today.

When I **go** to Grandma's house,
I **do** enjoy myself.
We always read the brand-new book
I **see** upon her shelf.

(chorus)

When I **went** last week to visit,
We **did** something new.
We worked out in her garden,
And we **saw** a movie, too.

(chorus)

© Harcourt

Helpers

(chorus) The helping verbs **has**, **have**, and **had**
Must have another one
To tell what happened when
Or tell how it was done.

The teacher **has helped** us
To learn what to say.
We **have made** costumes
To wear in our play.

(chorus)

The lines **were** learned.
We **had painted** the set.
We all said that this was
Our best play yet!

(chorus)

© Harcourt

How and Where

(chorus)

Use adverbs to tell **how**.
Use adverbs to tell **where**.
Use adverbs to tell how it was
That something happened there.

Where Jack's mother threw some seeds,
A beanstalk **quickly** grew.
Jack soon climbed to the top of it
Up to the clouds and through.

(chorus)

Nearby he saw a castle.
He tiptoed through the door,
And **nervously** he hid
When he heard a giant roar!

(chorus)

Grammar Jingles™ • Primary

♪♪ Letters Out, Apostrophes In ♪♪

(chorus)   A **contraction** is useful in writing.
You use two words to make one.
A letter goes out, an **apostrophe** in,
And then the word is done.

I've heard **it's** very pleasant
To play out in the snow,
But it **doesn't** snow where I live,
So I guess **I'll** never know.

(chorus)

I **can't** imagine living
Where **there's** swimming every day
And **I'd** never wear a snowsuit
When I went outside to play.

(chorus)

First, Next, Last

(chorus)   Think of a series of happenings,
             One and two and three.
             Use the words **First**, **Next**, and **Last**
             To tell the tale to me.

             First, I put on all my clothes.
             Next, I make my bed.
             Last, I tidy up my room
             Just like my mother said.

                      (chorus)

             First, I fix my cereal.
             Next, I get a spoon.
             Last, I quickly eat it up
             Because I'll be leaving soon.

                      (chorus)

Pause Here

Commas can be useful
For words all in a row.
Should I pause while reading?
They help the reader know.

First, you rake the soil.
Add water, seeds, and sun.
Then, watch for sprouts to grow.
Gardening is fun.

(chorus)

I planted pretty flowers—
Yellow, blue, and red.
If they do well, next week I'll plant
Some vegetables instead.

(chorus)

Two, Too, To

(chorus) A word that you are using
May not be what you thought.
When you see some words, they're different.
When you say them, they are not.

I **s-e-w** with thread.
I **s-o** like to read.
And here's one more that sounds like that—
I **s-o-w** a seed.

(chorus)

My sister likes the library.
I like **to** go there, **too**.
She likes to take **two** books **to** read,
And I take **two** books, **too**.

(chorus)

Susan Little (words and music) enjoys composing music and writing for young children. Her first song book was created especially for her kindergarten students, as were her first stories and games. After many years as a teacher and administrator, she became a developer and editor of educational materials. She now lives and writes in New Hampshire.

Dax Baumgartner (music and production) has been involved in music since he was very young. Playing piano since age 3, this Illinois native won three consecutive Junior World Piano Championships at ages 10, 11, and 12. Performing professionally since then, he joined vocal group 'N Sync's world tour as keyboardist at age 19 and toured with them for two years. He now operates his own music production company and recording studio in Florida.

Singers: Alex Acosta, Jenie Ashbaugh, Naijah Ashbaugh, Dax Baumgartner, Taylor Davey, Colleen DeFeo, Avery Ford, Molly Ford, Lauren Friedman, Erik Garbus, Chautauqua Kimble, Andi Mans, Scott McKenzie, Emily Morton, Nicholas Obrzut, Jenn Raymond, Jenica Tutin, Ashley Wood